Yellowsto
Travel Guide

Nature's Wonderland in Every Season

Henry Brew

Copyright

Contents

CHAPTER 1: INTRODUCTION

Welcome to Yellowstone National Park

Yellowstone National Park, the world's first National Park, is a popular destination for millions of visitors each year. Situated in the western United States, it features dense forests, hot springs, canyons, geysers, and rushing rivers, as well as the largest high-altitude lake in North America. The park is home to an immense amount of wildlife, including bison, elk, bears, 322 species of birds, and the gray wolf. With over 2,000 campsites, Yellowstone is a popular tourist attraction, especially for the erupting Old Faithful geyser.

The park is a super-volcano with over 10,000 hydrothermal features, and it experiences around 1,000-3,000 earthquakes annually. The geyser, known for its predictability, erupts every 92 minutes on average. Over 4 million visitors visit the park annually.

Some of the best residents of Yellowstone include bison jams, grizzly bears, whistle pigs, speedy birds, and boreal chorus frogs. Bison jams occur when cars wait for bison to cross the road, while grizzly bears use their large humps to dig for roots and insects. Whistling pigs warn their family and friends about potential threats, while the Peregrine falcon can dive at over 200 mph when catching prey midair.

Yellowstone National Park is a popular destination for tourists, with a rich wildlife and a variety of wildlife.

Overview of the park's significance and unique features

Significance

Yellowstone is the heart of the Greater Yellowstone Ecosystem, one of the world's last and biggest largely intact natural ecosystems. With over 10,000 hydrothermal sites and half of the world's active geysers, Yellowstone contains the most active, diversified, and undamaged collection of combined geothermal phenomena. The park is also rich in cultural and historical treasures, including 25 National Register of Historic Places monuments, landmarks, and districts.

Distinct characteristics

Yellowstone National Park, located on top of a dormant volcano, has more geysers and hot springs than any other area on the planet. This genuinely unique national park is filled with wonders, from the Yellowstone Grand Canyon to fauna such as America's biggest buffalo herd, grizzly bears, and wolves. Yellowstone National Park has over half of the world's hydrothermal features, generating an appearance that makes the earth seem to be on fire. Old Faithful, the most renowned of the geysers, is one of the most popular and known natural marvels in the United States.

Special considerations for visitors

Yellowstone National Park is a pristine wilderness, and visitors play a crucial role in preserving its delicate ecosystem. To ensure a positive experience, visitors should follow Leave No Trace principles, stay on designated trails, and refrain from disturbing wildlife, and dispose of waste properly. Participate in organized clean-up events to contribute to the park's conservation efforts.

Safety guidelines for wildlife encounters are essential, especially when observing diverse species like bison, elk, bears, and wolves. Maintain a safe distance, avoid feeding wildlife, and store food securely to avoid attracting them to your campsite. Stay informed about park-specific considerations, such as trail closures, construction activities, or weather conditions, and stay connected with park authorities through visitor centers, ranger stations, and official communication channels.

Respect for geothermal features, such as geysers and hot springs, and follow designated boardwalks and pathways when exploring these areas. Be prepared for sudden temperature fluctuations and take it slow if not acclimated to higher altitudes. Check the weather forecast regularly for outdoor activities.

Respect the cultural and historical significance of Yellowstone, especially concerning Native American heritage. Follow guidelines for visiting sacred sites and be aware of cultural sensitivities. Engage with educational programs offered by the park to deepen your understanding of the cultural richness intertwined with the landscape.

Sustainable transportation options within the park, such as the shuttle system or electric vehicle charging stations, can help reduce carbon footprints. By embracing these special considerations, visitors can enhance their Yellowstone experience while contributing to the park's conservation goals.

CHAPTER 2: GETTING TO YELLOWSTONE

Transportation options (airports, roads, etc.)

IMPROVING YOUR YELLOWSTONE EXPERIENCE: TRANSPORTATION

Traveling to and within West Yellowstone might be difficult at times, but the stunning beauty and unforgettable experiences that await you are well worth the effort. When you plan out how to get here and how to move about, you may turn a decent vacation into an extraordinary one.

This guide includes vital information for getting to West Yellowstone and exploring its environs. Discover helpful hints for making your travel easier. These pointers will help you fully appreciate the breathtaking scenery and different activities that this location has to offer.

- ➢ Flying over Here

- ➢ Driving Directions

- ➢ Arriving

- ➢ Exploring

FLIGHT HERE

There are a few alternatives for flying into West Yellowstone but always contact ahead for transportation once you arrive.

- • **Yellowstone International Airport**

West Yellowstone's nearest and most convenient airport is Yellowstone Airport (WYS). It is just a few miles from West Yellowstone and is open from mid-May to mid-October when it is busiest. Sky West Airlines operates flights for Delta Air Lines and United Airlines. You'll have all you need and be exploring nature in no time with several rental car businesses at the airport and other local accommodation options. If you want to hire a car, make a reservation in advance since cars are limited.

- **Yellowstone International Airport is located in Bozeman, Montana.**

Bozeman Yellowstone International Airport (BZN) is the nearest year-round airport to West Yellowstone. BZN, the busiest airport near Yellowstone, offers nonstop flights to more than 20 locations in the United States, as well as links to destinations all over the globe. This airport is 90 miles north of West Yellowstone, so you'll need to make additional transport arrangements with a neighboring shuttle, taxi, or car rental business to get to West Yellowstone. Although the drive from Bozeman to Yellowstone may add to your long day of travel, the scenery will be breathtaking and the destination will be immensely rewarding.

- **Idaho Falls Regional Airport is situated in the city of Idaho Falls, Idaho.**

Another alternative for year-round travel to West Yellowstone is Idaho Falls Regional Airport (IDA). Because the airport is 110 miles south of West Yellowstone, plan your trip from the airport to West Yellowstone before landing. IDA offers nonstop flights from 13 different locations in the United States, including Las Vegas, Dallas/Fort Worth, Denver, and Oakland, California.

- **GETTING HERE BY CAR**

From the city of Salt Lake City, Utah

Take I-15 N for 213 miles to Idaho Falls, Idaho. Take the ramp to the RIGHT to US-20 E at exit 119.

Take US-20 E for roughly 110 miles from Idaho Falls, Idaho.

Montana's Bozeman

Take US-191 S for about 90 miles.

Grand Teton National Park and Jackson Hole, Wyoming

WY-22 W will take you 17.1 miles across the Teton Pass in Idaho. Continue on ID-33 NW for another 23.9 miles. Turn RIGHT (north) onto ID-32 and go 28.4 miles to Ashton. Turn RIGHT (north) onto US-20 E and continue for 37 miles to West Yellowstone.

- **Year-Round Driving Advice:**

Always use turnouts to let others pass. No trash. Watch for animals on the road in the winter.

Drive slowly since the roads may be snow-packed and slick.

From November to April, always have chains on hand.

Keep your petrol tank and windshield wiper fluid topped up this summer.

To avoid overheating, turn off the air conditioner.

Stay hydrated by drinking lots of water.

- **SHUTTLES, BUSES, AND MORE ARRIVE IN WEST YELLOWSTONE**

Whether you fly into one of the more handy airports or from a neighboring city such as Salt Lake City, you'll require transportation from the airport to your West Yellowstone lodgings. Several firms can make traveling simple, eliminating the need for a rental car— but be sure to contact ahead to learn about what's available during your trip.

➢ Bus/Shuttle

Several operators provide bus and shuttle services to and from airports in Bozeman, Montana, Idaho Falls, Idaho, and Salt Lake City, Utah. Reservations are essential, and there are costs. In the summer, local shuttles may transport visitors from the West Yellowstone region to Yellowstone Park trailheads, while in the winter, snow coaches can transport visitors.

Taxi service is offered in West Yellowstone and to drop-off sites across Yellowstone Park all year. Reservations are necessary.

- **WEST YELLOWSTONE EXPLORATION: RENTAL CARS AND MORE**

Once you've arrived in West Yellowstone, you'll need a way to travel about so you can see all of the sites and participate in all of the unique activities Yellowstone has to offer. You may discover shuttle services to assist you in exploring the region without the added cost of a rental vehicle; nevertheless, hiring a car can optimize your flexibility for exploration during your Yellowstone journey.

> Automobile Rentals

Rental automobiles are available in West Yellowstone on a seasonal basis at a variety of sites, including the Yellowstone airport and local businesses. You may also look for automobile rentals on websites like Turo.

> Tours with a Guide

Tours into Yellowstone Park and the Grand Teton National Park/Jackson region are available throughout the summer months via park-approved tour companies. Snow bus or snowmobile rides into Yellowstone Park and the Custer Gallatin National Forest are available.

Nearest major cities and their proximity

- Montana's Bozeman:

Bozeman is roughly 90 miles north of Yellowstone National Park.

Travel Time: Depending on traffic and road conditions, the travel from Bozeman to the park's North Entrance takes around 1.5 to 2 hours.

Bozeman has a dynamic downtown, and cultural attractions, and is the entrance to the picturesque Gallatin Valley.

- Wyoming's Jackson

Jackson is about 56 miles south of Yellowstone.

Travel Time: The drive from Jackson to the park's South Entrance takes around 1 to 1.5 hours, going via Grand Teton National Park.

Jackson is well-known for its attractive town center, outdoor activity, and proximity to Grand Teton National Park.

- Wyoming's Cody

Cody is roughly 52 miles east of Yellowstone National Park.

Travel Time: The travel from Cody to the park's East Entrance takes around 1 to 1.5 hours on average.

Cody is well-known for its rodeo activities, the Buffalo Bill Center of the West, and its ties to the history of the American West.

- West Yellowstone National Park, Montana

West Yellowstone is located right outside the West Entrance.

Travel Time: The town is just close to the park, making it simple to see Yellowstone's attractions.

Notable Features: West Yellowstone serves as a major tourist base, providing lodging, eating, and recreational opportunities.

- Gardiner, Montana

Gardiner is situated near the park's North Entrance.

Travel Time: Gardiner serves as a gateway to the Mammoth Hot Springs region and is near the famous Roosevelt Arch.

Notable Features: Gardiner, with its small-town charm and attractive surroundings, serves as a pleasant gateway to the park.

Understanding the closeness of these major cities to Yellowstone is critical for planning travel itineraries and deciding on access points.

Each community has its own distinct attractions, allowing for exploration and cultural experiences before or after immersing oneself in the marvels of Yellowstone National Park.

Driving tips and routes

Before embarking on your Yellowstone National Park journey, check the official website or contact the park's visitor centers for current road conditions and closures. Respect posted speed limits to enhance safety and protect wildlife, especially in wildlife-rich areas. Know your park's five entrance points and fees, and consider purchasing an annual pass for multiple visits. Plan your route to include iconic scenic drives like the Grand Loop Road and be aware of key points of interest along the way.

Ensure sufficient fuel is available before entering the park, as fueling stations are limited within Yellowstone. Use pullouts to allow faster traffic to pass and enjoy scenic views without obstructing traffic flow. Be prepared for unpredictable weather by packing essentials like warm clothing, blankets, and a first aid kit. Maintain a safe distance from wildlife and use pullouts for viewing.

When driving an RV or towing a trailer, be aware of size restrictions on certain roads and plan your route accordingly.

Avoid driving during dawn and dusk, as wildlife is more active at these times. Have an emergency kit in your vehicle, including water, non-perishable snacks, a flashlight, and basic tools. Be self-sufficient and familiarize yourself with available roadside assistance services, especially if traveling in more remote areas of the park. By following these driving tips and being mindful of road conditions, wildlife, and safety, you can make the most of your Yellowstone National Park journey.

CHAPTER 3: PARK OVERVIEW

Size and geographical features

- **Park Dimensions**

Yellowstone National Park is one of the biggest national parks in the United States, spanning an astonishing 2.2 million acres.

- **Various Landscapes**

Yellowstone has a wide variety of scenery, including:

> ➢ Mountains: The Absaroka Range, Gallatin Range, and Beartooth Mountains are all included in the park.

- ➢ Lakes: Yellowstone Lake, North America's biggest high-altitude lake, is a noteworthy feature.
- ➢ Rivers and Waterfalls: The Yellowstone River runs through the park, producing spectacular waterfalls such as the Lower and Upper Falls in the Yellowstone Grand Canyon.
- ➢ Valleys and Meadows: The Lamar and Hayden valleys have large meadows where animals congregate.

Yellowstone is located on a volcanic hotspot, which has resulted in geothermal phenomena such as geysers, hot springs, and mud pots.

- ▪ **Yellowstone Caldera**

The Yellowstone Caldera, a large volcanic crater produced by a succession of violent volcanic eruptions, sits in the heart of the park. This caldera is a distinctive geological feature of the park, contributing to its distinct and dynamic ecosystem.

- ▪ **Hydrothermal Characteristics**

Yellowstone National Park has approximately 10,000 hydrothermal phenomena, including the world-famous Old Faithful geyser, Grand Prismatic Spring, and Fountain Paint Pots. These geothermal marvels provide witness to the park's dynamic volcanic past.

- **Variation in Altitude**

The park's elevation varies from around 5,282 feet (1,610 meters) at Reese Creek to 11,358 feet (3,462 meters) at Eagle Peak. Depending on where they are in the park, visitors may encounter a variety of climates and temperatures.

- **Wilderness Reserves**

Yellowstone National Park has large wilderness regions that support a broad diversity of animals, including grizzly bears, wolves, elk, bison, and many bird species.

- **Geological Structures**

The park has impressive geological structures, such as petrified trees in the Specimen Ridge region and the multicolored rock formations of the Yellowstone Grand Canyon.

Overview of the park's history and establishment

Yellowstone National Park, once inhabited by Indigenous peoples like the Shoshone, Crow, Bannock, and Nez Perce, began its exploration in the early 19th century. The Lewis and Clark Expedition of 1804-1806 provided initial insights, but more comprehensive exploration occurred in the 1870s.

The Washburn Expedition, led by Henry Washburn, explored the region and advocated for the creation of a national park.

In 1872, Yellowstone National Park was established when President Ulysses S. Grant signed the Act of Dedication. Geologist Ferdinand V. Hayden played a crucial role in advocating for the park's protection, with his surveys and documentation of its geological features contributing significantly to its establishment.

The U.S. Army administered Yellowstone to protect it from threats like poaching and vandalism, with Fort Yellowstone established. The National Park Service (NPS) Era, created in 1916, focused on conservation, visitor services, and environmental protection. Yellowstone was designated a UNESCO World Heritage Site in 1978, recognizing its exceptional natural features and global ecological importance.

Over the years, Yellowstone has faced challenges such as wildfires, wolf reintroduction, and threats to its ecosystem. Conservation efforts, research, and public awareness initiatives have been vital in addressing these challenges.

Yellowstone also has cultural significance, with historic structures like the Old Faithful Inn and the Roosevelt Arch reflecting the architectural heritage of the early park era.

Biodiversity and notable wildlife

- Ecosystem Diversity

Yellowstone National Park is known for its various ecosystems, which include alpine meadows and coniferous forests, as well as geothermal sites and vast grasslands. This range of ecosystems adds to the park's tremendous biodiversity.

- Famous Megafauna

Bison (Bison bison): Yellowstone National Park is home to the last wild herd of American bison. These distinctive species are often sighted in the Lamar and Hayden Valleys of the park.

Elk (Cervus canadensis): Elk are plentiful in Yellowstone, particularly in the north and west. The bugling of elk resonates across the valleys during the autumn rut.

Grizzly Bears (Ursus arctos horribilis): Yellowstone National Park is an important habitat for grizzly bears. These magnificent beasts may be seen throughout the park, especially in the backcountry.

Gray Wolves (Canis lupus): The reintroduction of gray wolves to Yellowstone National Park in the 1990s was a watershed moment in conservation. The Lamar Valley is an excellent spot for wolf viewing.

Pronghorn (Antilocapra americana): The park's grasslands and sagebrush sections are home to pronghorn, also known as American antelope.

- Dog Predators

Coyotes (Canis latrans): Coyotes are versatile predators that may be found all across the park. They play an important function in the ecology by controlling rodent numbers.

- Avian Varieties

With almost 300 bird species documented, Yellowstone is a birder's paradise. Bald eagles, ospreys, trumpeter swans, sandhill cranes, and a variety of waterfowl are among the notable species.

- Marine Life

Yellowstone Lake and its tributaries are home to Yellowstone cutthroat trout, which contribute to the park's aquatic biodiversity.

- Reptiles and Amphibians

While reptiles and amphibians are less visible, species such as garter snakes, Western toads, and chorus frogs contribute to the overall biodiversity of the area.

- Efforts to Conserve Biodiversity

Yellowstone conservation efforts are aimed at maintaining the park's biodiversity. To preserve the fragile balance of the environment, efforts include habitat restoration, important species monitoring, and invasive species management.

- Wildlife Observation and Ethics

Visitors may see wildlife responsibly by keeping a safe distance, utilizing binoculars or telephoto lenses for close-ups, and according to park restrictions. To prevent problems, "wildlife jams" that can develop when animals are near highways should be avoided.

Yellowstone's richness reflects its status as a protected natural refuge. The park's conservation efforts guarantee that future generations will be able to enjoy the beauty and biological diversity of its varied flora and wildlife.

CHAPTER 4: WEATHER AND CLIMATE

Seasonal variations

- **Spring lasts from April until June.**

Warming temperatures herald the arrival of spring in the park. Temperatures throughout the day vary from 30°F to 60°F (-1°C to 16°C).

Wildlife: Many animals give birth in the spring. Calves of bison and elk may be seen. The activity of bears and other animals increases.

Meadows are bursting with bright wildflowers, creating a beautiful scene.

Low visitor numbers make it perfect for hiking and animal viewing. Snow may have caused certain places and routes to remain closed.

- **Summer lasts from July until August.**

Summer provides hot weather, with daily highs ranging from 70°F to 80°F (21°C to 27°C). The evenings are colder.

- ➢ Animal: There is a lot of animal activity, including bear sightings. In meadows, you may readily identify bison and elk.

> Wildflowers: The Park's picturesque appeal is enhanced by the continued display of wildflowers.

Tourist season is in full swing. All roads and infrastructure are operational. Popular activities include hiking, camping, and boating.

- **Autumn: September to October**

Daytime temperatures range from 30°F to 60°F (-1°C to 16°C) due to the crisp fall air. The nights are cold.

Elk rutting season, when males bugle to attract mates. Bison and other animals are preparing for the winter.

Aspen trees turn golden in the autumn, giving a magnificent display of leaves.

> Activities: There are fewer visitors than during the summer. This is a fantastic time to photograph animals and enjoy the fall foliage. Some facilities may have to shut down.

- **Winter lasts from November to March.**

The weather in winter is frigid, with daytime highs ranging from 0°F to 20°F (-18°C to -7°C). Temperatures below zero are not unusual.

Wildlife: Herds of bison and elk migrate to lower altitudes. Wolves and other predators have increased their activity.

Heavy snowfall turns the park into a winter paradise. Geothermal features produce a lot of steam in the chilly air.

Access to activities is restricted. There are snow coach and snowmobile trips available. In approved locations, cross-country skiing and snowshoeing are popular activities. It is still feasible to see wildlife.

- **Seasonal Considerations:**

Road Closures: Due to snow or maintenance, several roads and facilities may be closed during the shoulder seasons (spring and autumn).

- ➢ Numbers of Visitors: Summer has the most visitors, while winter has the fewest.
- ➢ Clothing: Throughout the year, layers are required. Cold-weather clothing is required in the winter.
- ➢ Animal Safety: Always adhere to animal safety precautions, particularly during the spring calving and autumn rutting seasons.

Understanding Yellowstone's seasonal fluctuations is critical for organizing a vacation that corresponds with personal tastes, intended activities, and the unique experiences each season provides.

Best times to visit based on weather preferences

- **Late spring (May to Early June) for mild weather and wildflowers**

Late spring weather is milder, with daytime highs ranging from 50°F to 70°F (10°C to 21°C). Evenings may still be chilly.

Colorful wildflowers are in full bloom across the park, providing a lovely environment.

Activities: Excellent for hiking, animal observation, and taking in the splendor of spring. There may still be snow in certain locations, so verify road and trail conditions.

- **Hot Days and Peak Mid-Summer (July to August) Wildlife Activity**

Weather: The hottest months are midsummer, with daily highs ranging from 70°F to 80°F (21°C to 27°C). Evenings are enjoyable.

- Animal: There is a lot of animal activity, such as bears, elk, and bison. During the peak season, the park is alive with life.
- Activities: All roads and facilities are available, allowing for a variety of activities ranging from hiking to boating. Summer crowds are at their peak.

- **Early fall (September to early October) is best for fall foliage and elk rutting.**

Temperatures drop in the fall, with daytime highs ranging from 30°F to 60°F (-1°C to 16°C). The nights may be cold.

Aspen trees turn golden in the autumn, giving a magnificent display of leaves.

Elk rutting season has begun, with males bugling. Bison and other animals are preparing for the winter.

Fall is wonderful for fewer people, animal photography, and taking in the changing hues. Some facilities may close as early as October.

- **Mid-winter (January to February) for Winter Wonderland and Unique Geothermal Displays**

Winter days are frigid, with highs ranging from 0°F to 20°F (-18°C to -7°C). Temperatures below zero are not unusual.

➢ Snowfall: When it snows heavily, the park is transformed into a winter wonderland. Geothermal features produce a lot of steam in the chilly air.

Winter enthusiasts may enjoy snow coach and snowmobile rides, cross-country skiing, and snowshoeing despite the limited accessibility. It is still feasible to see wildlife.

- **Overarching Considerations:**
➢ Crowds: Summer (mid-June to August) has the most visitors. Visit during the shoulder seasons (spring and autumn) to avoid crowds.
➢ Road Closures: During the shoulder seasons and winter, several roads may be blocked owing to snow, limiting access to particular locations.

Choosing the ideal time to visit Yellowstone based on weather preferences enables guests to customize their experience depending on the activities they want and the temperature they prefer. Every season provides a different perspective on the park's natural splendor.

Packing recommendations

Yellowstone National Park offers a variety of seasons, making packing essential for visitors. Layered clothing, comfortable footwear, hats and sunglasses, sunscreen, a reusable water bottle, and a daypack are essential for all seasons. Season-specific items include a light jacket or fleece for cool mornings and evenings, lightweight clothing for warmer temperatures, binoculars for wildlife viewing, and bug repellent for mosquitoes. Warmer layers, such as jackets and coats, are recommended for cooler days. Cold-weather gear, such as insulated boots, warm gloves, and a winter jacket, is essential for winter activities. Hand warmers are especially useful during cold winter days.

Miscellaneous items include a camera, map, guidebook, first aid kit, and power bank. Bear spray, backpack rain cover, and reusable utensils and snack containers are also important for bear country hikes. Winter-specific items include snow gear, waterproof boots insulated clothing, and traction devices for icy or snowy surfaces.

To ensure a smooth trip, check park alerts, road closures, and weather advisories before your trip. Plan for limited connectivity in some areas, as mobile reception is limited in some areas.

By packing thoughtfully and considering seasonal variations, visitors can prepare for the unique conditions and experiences Yellowstone National Park offers throughout the year.

CHAPTER 5: ACCOMMODATIONS

Lodges and campgrounds within the park

Yellowstone National Park offers a variety of camping options, from car camping paradise to remote backcountry sites and RV heaven. Campgrounds can be reserved in advance during peak summer months through Yellowstone National Park Lodges or the National Park Service at recreation.gov. Some popular campgrounds include Bridge Bay, Canyon, Fishing Bridge RV Park, Grant Village, Indian Creek, Lewis Lake, Madison, Mammoth, Norris, Pebble Creek, Slough Creek, and Tower Fall.

Mammoth Campground is located near the park's North Entrance and is a great place to relax and spot bison or elk. It is close to Mammoth Hot Springs, offering live entertainment in the form of ranger programs in the amphitheater. The park's only year-round campground, sites can be reserved through recreation.gov from April 1 to October 15 and are first-come, first-served the rest of the year. Each site has a picnic table, fire pit with grate, flush toilets, and water pumps with potable water.

Indian Creek Campground is located at the base of the Gallatin Mountains and offers stunning views and access to hiking and fishing. It is usually open from early June through early September and has several sites that can accommodate RVs up to 35 feet in length. The restrooms are vault toilets and can be reserved through recreation.gov.

Madison Campground is the nearest to the West Entrance of Yellowstone National Park and the hamlet of West Yellowstone, Montana. It's close to the Madison River and a fantastic place to see elk and bison herds. Madison is a fantastic alternative for RVers, with pull-through and back-in sites for rigs up to 40 feet in length and a seasonal dump station open from early May to mid-October each year. Generators are permitted at this campsite throughout the day from 8 a.m. to 8 p.m.

To find the perfect campground, consider checking the park's website and checking the availability of facilities and amenities.

Yellowstone National Park offers various camping options for visitors to the park. Some of the most popular options include Norris Campground, Canyon Campground, Bridge Bay Campground, Fishing Bridge RV Park, and Grant Village Campground.

Norris Campground is located near the Norris Geyser Basin, offering easy access to some of the world's most incredible geysers and flush toilets. It is open from late May through late September and has 112 sites, with seven of them being for RVs. Each site has a picnic table and fire pit, and guests can walk to the Museum of the National Park Ranger from the campground. Reservations must be booked at least 13 months in advance.

Canyon Campground is an excellent choice for those wanting to experience the beauty of the Grand Canyon of the Yellowstone River. Located in a lodge pole pine forest in Canyon Village, it offers flush toilets, hot showers, potable drinking water, and laundry facilities. RVers can also access the internet from nearby lodges.

Bridge Bay Campground is one of the parks largest with 432 campsites, offering flush toilets and sinks with running water for modern comforts while enjoying outstanding views of Yellowstone Lake and the Absaroka mountain range. The sites can accommodate rigs up to 40 feet long, and there is a seasonal disposal station on-site.

Fishing Bridge RV Park is the only Yellowstone campground in the park with full hookups and a dump station. It underwent a major renovation in 2021, including bigger campsites and remodeled shower and laundry facilities. The campground is located on the eastern side of the park, across the road from the historic Fishing Bridge Museum and Visitor Center. Nightly evening ranger programs at the visitor center's amphitheater are held from June through early September.

Grant Village Campground is another option for camping near Yellowstone's South Entrance. It is open from late May through early October and requires reservations. The campground is located in the heart of grizzly country, allowing hard-sided campers to bond with fellow RVers. Its 310 sites can accommodate RVs up to 40 feet long in most cases and up to 95 feet in certain cases.

Guests can take a shower, use the flush toilets, and do laundry at the campground, but leave their campfire supplies at home. From late May until early October, the RV Park is normally open.

Grant Village, located on the southwest shore of Yellowstone Lake, is open from early June to early September and offers flush toilets, running water, pay showers, laundry facilities, and a seasonal dump station. It is a great choice for those looking to explore both Yellowstone and Grand Teton National Parks.

Lewis Lake Campground is the furthest south of Yellowstone's campgrounds and is a peaceful spot for tent campers. Generators are not allowed, and only RVs smaller than 25 feet in length can be accommodated. The campground has vault toilets but offers seasonal potable water.

Pebble Creek Campground, located near the park's Northeast Entrance, is home to 27 sites and is close to sunrise explorations of Lamar Valley. It has vault toilets and no generator use. Sites can be reserved through

Slough Creek Campground, the smallest in the park, is home to 16 sites and is located between Lamar Valley and Tower-Roosevelt. It is situated along the picturesque Slough Creek in a sage meadow and is close to some of the best wildlife viewing in Yellowstone. Clean pit toilets and a water pumping station are available, but generators are prohibited.

Lodging within the park

- **Cabins and Canyon Lodge**

Location: Canyon Lodge and Cabins is located at 41 Clover Ln in Yellowstone National Park, Wyoming.

Canyon Lodge and Cottages is a huge complex with over 500 rooms and cottages, offering the greatest accommodations in Yellowstone. Canyon Lodge, located on the park's east side near the Grand Canyon of the Yellowstone River, is open from early June to early October. A two-year hotel refurbishment was completed in 2016, resulting in five new lodges and 400-plus guest rooms, including 2-Bedroom Suites, Superior Lodge Rooms, and Standard Lodge Rooms. The five new lodges are all LEED-certified. In 2017, the main public structure, which includes the eateries and gift store, was refurbished and reopened.

Amenities provided by the property

Parking is free.

Internet service for a fee

Restaurant

Hiking

- **Cabins at Lake Lodge**
  ➢ Location: Yellowstone National Park, 459 Lake Village Rd, WY 82190

Lake Lodge Cabins has a main lodge with a spacious porch and a rocking chair view of Yellowstone Lake. The main lodge is made of logs and serves as the focal point of this traditional and pleasant structure. 186 cabins with private bathrooms are available behind the resort in freshly remodeled Western and Frontier designs, as well as the basic Pioneer cabins. Lake Lodge is open from early June until late September. The main lodge has a charming lobby with two fireplaces, a lounge, and a gift shop that cordially invites travelers to stop and speak.

Amenities provided by the property

Parking is free.

A bar or a lounge

Restaurant

Fishing while hiking

The gift store

Hotel that does not allow smoking

Area for picnicking

Snow Lodge & Cabins at Old Faithful

> ➤ Location: Yellowstone National Park, WY 82190, 2051 Snow Lodge Ave

The Snow Lodge, which opened in 1999, is the newest of the park's full-service hotels and has received the Cody Award for Western Design as well as Travel and Leisure's Inn of the Month. The Snow Lodge's massive wood structure, outside log columns, and cedar shingle roof are all part of the design that will make it a prominent example of traditional "architecture." In addition, the Snow Lodge has a full-service dining room, a quick-service "Geyser Grill," and the beautiful Bear Den Gift Store.

Make suggestions for changes to what we present.

Enhance this listing

Amenities provided by the property

Parking is free.

Internet service for a fee

Internet access Bar/lounge Restaurant

Nearby hotels and accommodation

Some of the nearby options include the Yellowstone Park Hotel in West Yellowstone, Montana, which offers modern amenities, free Wi-Fi, and proximity to shops and attractions. Other options include the Explorer Cabins at Yellowstone, a rustic-style lodge with kitchenettes, outdoor seating, and convenient access to the park. The Three Bear Lodge, a family-friendly Western-themed lodge, offers an on-site restaurant and indoor pool.

In Gardiner, Montana, the Roosevelt Hotel offers a historic ambiance and modern comforts, with on-site dining, free Wi-Fi, and scenic views of the surrounding mountains. Absaroka Lodge, a charming mountain lodge near the Yellowstone River, offers outdoor seating areas, river views, and a contemporary inn with well-appointed rooms.

In Cody, Wyoming, the Cody Cowboy Village offers Western-themed cabins with kitchenettes, outdoor seating, and a friendly cowboy atmosphere. The Cody Hotel offers modern rooms with a fitness center, on-site restaurant, and proximity to attractions. The Chamberlin Inn is a historic inn in downtown Cody, offering elegant rooms, a garden courtyard, and easy access to local shops and restaurants.

In Jackson, Wyoming, the Wort Hotel combines luxury with Western charm, offering fine dining, spa services, and proximity to the town square. Rusty Parrot Lodge and Spa is a boutique lodge with a focus on luxury and personalized service, offering an on-site spa, an award-winning restaurant, and upscale accommodations. Finally, SpringHill Suites by Marriott Jackson Hole is a contemporary hotel with spacious suites and amenities.

Reservation tips and considerations

Yellowstone National Park offers a variety of lodging options, including lodges, camping, and other accommodations. To ensure a smooth and enjoyable visit, it is essential to make reservations early, be flexible, and consider shoulder seasons for fewer crowds and more lodging options. If your preferred lodge is fully booked, explore options at different locations within the park.

Campgrounds within Yellowstone also require reservations, so plan and check the National Park Service website for availability. Nearby hotels must also make early reservations, as they fill up quickly, especially during peak season. Understanding cancellation policies and package deals can help save costs compared to booking each component separately.

If your preferred hotel is fully booked, explore alternative accommodations such as bed and breakfasts, vacation rentals, or cabins. Campground reservations should be made as early as possible, especially during peak season. Backcountry permits should be obtained and planned accordingly.

To make reservations, use the official Yellowstone National Park website or authorized booking platforms, and avoid third-party websites that may charge additional fees. Ensure accurate contact information when making reservations, coordinate group reservations, and stay informed by regularly checking the official website for updates and changes to reservation policies or availability.

Planning and reserving accommodations well in advance are crucial steps to ensure a smooth and enjoyable Yellowstone National Park visit.

CHAPTER 6: EXPLORING THE PARK

Highlights of key attractions (Old Faithful, Grand Canyon of the Yellowstone, etc.)

Yellowstone National Park is well-known for its breathtaking natural beauty and distinctive geothermal elements. Here are several highlights, including Old Faithful and the Yellowstone Grand Canyon:

> ➤ 1. Old Faithful Geyser: - Old Faithful is one of the world's most renowned geysers, famed for its dependability in erupting every 90 minutes. The magnificent steam and water column may reach heights of 100 to 180 feet.

- ➢ 2. Grand Canyon of the Yellowstone: The Yellowstone River built this amazing canyon, which has multicolored walls, breathtaking waterfalls, and picturesque vistas. Artists Point and Inspiration Point provide amazing canyon views.

- ➢ 3. Mammoth Hot Springs: A sequence of travertine terraces constructed by hot springs, displaying bright hues produced by thermophiles (heat-loving bacteria). Lower Terraces, Main Terraces, and Upper Terraces are the three main terraces.

- ➢ 4. Yellowstone Lake: - The biggest high-altitude lake in North America, encompassing over 130 square miles. - Offers boating, fishing, and stunning lakeside views.

- ➢ 5. Norris Geyser Basin: Contains a range of geothermal phenomena such as geysers, hot springs, and fumaroles. The highest active geyser in the world, Steamboat Geyser, is situated here.

➤ 6. Grand Prismatic Spring: - One of the world's biggest hot springs, famous for the vibrant and unique colors produced by thermophiles microorganisms. The bright colors are best seen from the raised promenade.

➤ 7. Hayden Valley: - A fantastic place to see animals, including bison, elk, grizzly bears, and wolves. The Yellowstone River runs through this beautiful valley.

➤ 8. West Thumb Geyser Basin: Located along Yellowstone Lake's shoreline, it mixes hydrothermal characteristics with a spectacular lakeside landscape. Hot springs, geysers, and the Abyss Pool are among the attractions.

➤ 9. Mount Washburn: A popular hiking site that provides panoramic views of the park. The walk leads to the peak, where a fire lookout provides amazing views.

➤ 10. Lamar Valley: Known as the "Serengeti of North America" due to its abundance of species such as bison, wolves, and pronghorn. It has beautiful vistas and is a wonderful place for animal photography.

These attractions are just a small portion of what Yellowstone National Park has to offer. The park is a natural wonderland, making it a must-see destination for nature lovers and outdoor enthusiasts.

Hiking trails and difficulty levels

Yellowstone National Park offers a variety of hiking trails to cater to different skill levels and preferences. Some notable trails include Uncle Tom's Trail, Mount Washburn Trail, Fairy Falls Trail, Lone Star Geyser Trail, Mystic Falls Trail, Wraith Falls Trail, Storm Point Trail, Artist Point Trail, Special Ridge Trail, and Avalanche Peak Trail.

Uncle Tom's Trail is moderate to strenuous, offering close-up views of the Lower Falls and over 300 metal stairs. Mount Washburn Trail offers panoramic views of Yellowstone from the summit, while Fairy Falls Trail is a relatively flat trail leading to the beautiful Fairy Falls. The Lone Star Geyser Trail is easy to moderate, with the geyser erupting approximately every three hours. Mystic Falls Trail takes hikers to the 70-foot Mystic Falls and offers views of the

Firehole River. Wraith Falls Trail is short and easy, suitable for all skill levels.

Storm Point Trail is located on the shores of Yellowstone Lake, offering scenic views and is suitable for all ages. Artist Point Trail offers breathtaking views of the Grand Canyon of the Yellowstone. Special Ridge Trail leads to Amethyst Mountain, offering expansive views and wildlife sightings. Avalanche Peak Trail ascends to the summit, providing panoramic views of surrounding mountains and Yellowstone Lake.

Scenic drives and viewpoints

A variety of scenic drives and viewpoints to showcase its diverse landscapes and abundant wildlife. The Grand Loop Road is the primary road system, connecting major attractions like the Upper Geyser Basin, Grand Canyon of the Yellowstone, and Mammoth Hot Springs. Firehole Canyon Drive is a short, scenic drive along the Firehole River, offering views of geysers and hot springs. Dunraven Pass connects Canyon Village and Tower Fall, offering breathtaking views of the surrounding mountains and wildlife. Norris to Mammoth Road passes through the scenic Gibbon River Canyon, offering views of Gibbon Falls. Lamar Valley is a must-visit for wildlife enthusiasts, offering excellent opportunities to view bison, elk, and wolves.

Yellowstone Lake Scenic Loop is a picturesque drive along the shores of Yellowstone Lake, offering views of the lake, mountains, and thermal features. The Beartooth Highway is a nearby scenic drive with stunning alpine scenery. Upper Terrace Drive (Mammoth Hot Springs) is a short loop that takes you to the Upper Terraces of Mammoth Hot Springs, offering unique views of the terraces and surrounding landscapes. Artist Point (South Rim Drive) in the Grand Canyon of Yellowstone offers a panoramic view of the canyon and Lower Falls. Hayden Valley Overlook is a prime spot for wildlife viewing, especially during early morning and evening.

CHAPTER 7: WILDLIFE VIEWING

Information on the park's diverse wildlife

Yellowstone National Park is a diverse ecosystem with over 300 bird species, including the largest free-roaming bison population in the world. The park also has a significant elk population, particularly in the northern range. Both grizzly bears and black bears inhabit the park, with grizzly bears more commonly found in the remote backcountry and black bears adaptable to various habitats.

Gray wolves reintroduced in the mid-1990s, are known for their presence in the Lamar Valley, often referred to as the "Serengeti of North America." Moose are present in the park, particularly in areas with wetlands and lakes, and are more commonly found in the southern part of Yellowstone. The pronghorn, the fastest land mammal in North America, can be spotted in open grasslands like Lamar Valley.

Bighorn sheep are adapted to the rugged terrain of the park and can be seen on rocky slopes, particularly in the Gardiner Canyon area. Mountain lions, solitary and preferring remote areas, inhabit the park. Coyotes are adaptable and can be seen hunting small mammals or scavenging.

Birdwatchers can observe over 300 bird species, including bald eagles, ospreys, trumpeter swans, and waterfowl. To ensure the safety of visitors and animals, approaching or feeding wildlife is prohibited in the park. Park regulations emphasize the importance of responsible wildlife viewing to maintain the integrity of this unique ecosystem.

Best locations and times for wildlife observation

Yellowstone National Park offers a unique opportunity to observe wildlife through its diverse ecosystems. Some of the best locations for wildlife observation include Lamar Valley, Hayden Valley, Mammoth Hot Springs Area, Old Faithful Area, Tower Fall Area, Gardiner Canyon, Norris Geyser Basin, Fishing Bridge Area, Bechler Region (Backcountry), and Pelican Valley.

Lamar Valley is known as the "Serengeti of North America" and is prime for wolf-watching, with bison, elk, and grizzly bears being common species. Hayden Valley is a hotspot for wildlife, especially bison, elk, and grizzly bears due to its wide-open spaces. The Mammoth Hot Springs Area attracts elk, particularly during the fall rut.

Old Faithful Area is located in the Southwestern part of the park, offering bison and elk sightings with thermal features. Tower Fall Area is in the Northeastern part of the park, with black bears, grizzly bears, and wolves often seen. Gardiner Canyon is in the Northern part near the North Entrance, with bighorn sheep often spotted on the rocky slopes.

Norris Geyser Basin is in the central part of the park, with elk and bison found in meadows around Norris Geyser Basin. The Fishing Bridge Area is in the Eastern part of the park, with waterfowl, otters, and sometimes grizzly bears spotted on the shores of Yellowstone Lake.

The Bechler Region (Backcountry) is in the Southwestern part of the park, offering opportunities to see moose, beavers, and other wildlife. Pelican Valley is renowned for its large bison herds.

To ensure a safe and enjoyable wildlife observation experience, it is essential to carry binoculars or a spotting scope and maintain a safe distance from wildlife.

Safety guidelines

Unique and diverse place with geothermal features, diverse wildlife, and varied terrain. To ensure safety, visitors should maintain distance from wildlife, avoid feeding animals, and stay in their vehicles when observing wildlife, carry bear spray, make noise when hiking, and hike in groups.

Geothermal features should be followed on boardwalks and trails, adhering to posted signs and warnings, and staying on designated paths when viewing geysers, hot springs, and other thermal features. Be cautious around rivers and lakes, as currents can be swift and unpredictable. Weather preparedness includes being ready for changing weather, altitude awareness, following speed limits, and finding safe pullouts to park vehicles.

Backcountry safety involves informing others about plans, carrying essentials, and knowing emergency services. Familiarize yourself with emergency contact numbers and the location of emergency services within the park, reporting incidents, accidents, or unsafe behavior to park rangers. Respect park rules and regulations to protect yourself, wildlife, and the environment, and educate yourself on Leave No Trace principles for responsible outdoor recreation.

By adhering to these safety guidelines, visitors can enjoy the unique and awe-inspiring features of Yellowstone National Park while minimizing risks and ensuring a safe experience for everyone.

CHAPTER 8: OUTDOOR ACTIVITIES

Fishing, boating, and other water activities

Park offers a variety of water activities for visitors to enjoy, including fishing, boating, canoeing and kayaking, swimming, and ice fishing. Fishing requires a valid permit, which can be obtained at park entrances or visitor centers. The park is home to native fish species such as cutthroat trout, Arctic grayling, and mountain whitefish. Popular fishing spots include Yellowstone Lake, Yellowstone River, Lamar River, Madison River, and Firehole River. Catch-and-release fishing is practiced in many areas to conserve fish populations.

Boating requires a free boat permit for motorized boats on Yellowstone Lake, while non-motorized boats like canoes, kayaks, and rowboats can be used without a permit. Boat launches are available at various locations, including Bridge Bay Marina, Grant Village, and Lewis Lake.

Canoeing and kayaking require no special permits and popular routes include Yellowstone Lake, Lewis Lake, and Shoshone Lake.

Safety is crucial, especially on large lakes, and appropriate gear should be worn. Rafting trips are available on sections of the Yellowstone River, but rafters must be aware of specific regulations and safety guidelines.

Swimming is limited due to cold water temperatures and potential thermal features in some areas. Designated swimming areas are available at Firehole River and Boiling River. Soaking in hot springs is strictly prohibited due to safety reasons. Boiling River is a popular spot where hot and cold waters mix, allowing swimming during designated hours.

Ice fishing is a popular winter activity on some park waters, including Yellowstone Lake and Lewis Lake. A valid fishing permit is required, and anglers should be aware of ice conditions and safety precautions.

Camping options and regulations

Camping options, including developed campgrounds, backcountry camping, and lodging options. Popular campgrounds include Madison, Bridge Bay, Canyon, Grant Village, and Mammoth.

Backcountry camping is available for a more secluded experience, but permits are required. Other lodging options include lodges, cabins, and hotels, with reservations highly recommended.

Campground and backcountry camping regulations include quiet hours, check-out times, and guidelines for food storage. Backcountry campers must follow Leave No Trace principles, pack out waste, and camp at designated sites. Reservations can be made in advance, especially during peak summer months, and can be made online through the Recreation.gov website.

RV and trailer camping sites are available at some campgrounds, while some offer limited electrical hookups. Group camping sites may have specific reservation requirements and restrictions. Campfire regulations include designated areas and backcountry stoves for cooking. Bear safety is also important, with many campgrounds providing bear-resistant food storage lockers.

Seasonal campground openings can vary due to weather conditions, and visitors should review regulations, obtain permits, and plan, especially during peak summer months when demand is high. Information on campground availability, regulations, and reservation options can be found on the official Yellowstone National Park website or at visitor centers within the park.

Winter activities (if applicable)

Park transforms into a snowy wonderland during winter, offering visitors unique opportunities to explore the park's geothermal features and wildlife. Winter activities include commercially guided snowmobile tours, snow coach tours, cross-country skiing, snowshoeing, ice fishing, wildlife watching, Lamar Valley wildlife viewing, geothermal features, winter lodging, and photography.

Snowmobile tours are available with specific regulations and reservations, while snow coach tours provide a comfortable way to explore the park's beauty. Cross-country skiing trails are available in some areas, while backcountry skiing is available for experienced skiers. Snowshoeing is allowed on many winter trails, and ranger-led programs offer educational insights into winter ecology. Ice fishing is allowed on some lakes during winter months, but regulations and safety guidelines must be followed.

Wildlife watching is an excellent time to observe winter wildlife, including wolves, elk, bison, and bighorn sheep. Lamar Valley is known for its winter wildlife, including wolves, with pullouts along the road for viewing. Geothermal features create a magical winter landscape with steamy landscapes from geysers and hot springs. Some lodges remain open during the winter season, providing a cozy and scenic accommodation option.

Photography opportunities are also available in the park's snow-covered landscapes and frosty trees. However, visitors should be prepared for cold temperatures, snow, and possible road closures, as some services and facilities may have limited availability during the winter season.

CHAPTER 9: VISITOR CENTERS AND MUSEUMS

Locations and services offered

It has vast and diverse landscape with various services and attractions. Key locations include the Old Faithful Area, which offers various services such as a Visitor Center, Old Faithful Inn, Old Faithful Lodge, restaurants, gift shops, and the famous Old Faithful Geyser. Activities include geysers, hot springs, boardwalks, and the Old Faithful Visitor Education Center.

Canyon Village offers hiking trails, viewpoints, and waterfalls. Mammoth Hot Springs offers thermal features, wildlife viewing, and the historic Fort Yellowstone. Yellowstone Lake Area offers boating, fishing, hiking, and scenic views. Norris Geyser Basin offers a museum, Norris Geyser Basin Information Center, and nearby Norris Campground.

Grant Village offers a Visitor Center, Grant Village Lodge, restaurants, gift shops, and the West Thumb Geyser Basin. Tower-Roosevelt Area offers Roosevelt Lodge, restaurants, gift shops, and the Tower Fall area. Lamar Valley offers wildlife viewing, especially for wolves, bison, and elk.

Fishing Bridge Area offers a Visitor Center, Fishing Bridge RV Park, and the historic Fishing Bridge Museum. West Yellowstone (outside the park) offers lodging, dining, shopping, and outdoor activities, including snowmobiling and proximity to Hebgen Lake. Backcountry Campgrounds and Trails offer primitive campsites with minimal facilities for backpacking, backcountry camping, and solitude in the wilderness.

Services may vary seasonally and are weather-dependent. Visitors are advised to check the official Yellowstone National Park website or contact park rangers for the latest information and updates.

Interpretive programs and ranger-led activities

It offers a variety of interpretive programs and ranger-led activities to enhance visitors' understanding and appreciation of the park's natural and cultural resources. These programs aim to educate and engage visitors while promoting responsible enjoyment of the park.

Some common interpretive programs include Ranger-Led Talks, Guided Walks, Evening Programs, Junior Ranger Programs, Themed Workshops, Wildlife Watching Tours, Campfire Programs, Snowshoe Walks (Winter), Photography Walks, and Art in the Park.

Ranger-led talks cover topics such as geology, wildlife, history, and thermal features, while guided walks cover topics like geothermal features, plant and animal life, and cultural history. Evening programs often feature presentations on astronomy, wildlife, or cultural history, with some programs including telescope viewing. Junior Ranger programs cater to younger visitors and involve educational activities, games, and booklets.

Themed workshops cover specific themes, such as birdwatching, photography, or tracking wildlife, and often require advance registration. Wildlife-watching tours focus on observing and learning about the park's diverse wildlife, with Lamar Valley being a popular location for wildlife tours. Campfire Programs include campfire talks, storytelling, and interactive activities. Snowshoe Walks provide insights into the park's winter ecology, while Photography Walks focus on capturing the beauty of Yellowstone's landscapes and wildlife. Art-focused programs may include plein-air painting sessions or nature sketching walks.

These ranger-led activities are typically included in the park entrance fee and can be found at visitor centers, ranger stations, and online.

Educational opportunities

Yellowstone National Park provides a variety of educational opportunities for visitors to deepen their understanding of the park's natural and cultural resources. These include visiting visitor centers with exhibits, interpretive displays, and knowledgeable rangers who can provide information on geology, wildlife, and history. Rangers conduct interpretive talks, walks, and programs on topics such as geothermal features, wildlife, and the park's cultural history. The Junior Ranger Program is geared towards children and encourages them to explore the park through educational activities.

The Yellowstone Forever Institute offers various educational programs, including field seminars, workshops, and custom programs led by expert instructors. Bookstores in the park, operated by the Yellowstone Forever Institute, offer educational books, maps, and other resources related to the park's natural and cultural history. Educational exhibits are featured in visitor centers and museums, while park newspapers and brochures provide informative articles, maps, and details about park resources.

Educational workshops and classes are offered by ranger-led programs and partner organizations, with some offering workshops and classes on birdwatching, photography, and tracking wildlife. Educational videos are also available at visitor centers, and themed interpretive trails are designed with interpretive signs to provide information about specific features.

Lamar Buffalo Ranch hosts classes and workshops focused on the park's wildlife, ecology, and conservation efforts. Educational outreach programs are offered in collaboration with educational institutions, aiming to enhance the visitor experience by fostering a deeper appreciation for the park's natural and cultural wonders.

CHAPTER 10: DINING AND SHOPPING

Restaurants and cafes within the park

Variety of dining options, including restaurants, cafeterias, and cafes, catering to different tastes and preferences. Some notable establishments include the Old Faithful Inn Dining Room, Old Faithful Snow Lodge Obsidian Dining Room, Canyon Village, Mammoth Hot Springs Dining Room, Terrace Grill, Lake Yellowstone Area, Grant Village, Tower-Roosevelt Area, Tower Fall General Store, Fishing Bridge Area, and Mammoth Hot Springs to Tower Area.

The Old Faithful Inn Dining Room offers breakfast, lunch, and dinner with views of Old Faithful. The Old Faithful Snow Lodge Obsidian Dining Room is a modern dining room with a focus on sustainable and regional ingredients. The Canyon Village Cafeteria offers casual dining with various food stations for quick meals. The Mammoth Hot Springs Dining Room serves breakfast, lunch, and dinner, while the Terrace Grill offers a casual setting with quick-service options near the Mammoth Hotel.

The Lake Yellowstone Area features the Lake Hotel Dining Room, Lake Lodge Deli, Grant Village Dining Room, Tower-Roosevelt Lodge Dining Room, Tower Fall General Store, Fishing Bridge General Store, and the Mammoth Hot Springs to Tower Area. The Roosevelt Cookout offers a unique dining experience with a cowboy-style cookout near Tower Roosevelt.

West Yellowstone, located outside the park's West Entrance, offers a range of restaurants, cafes, and diners. However, availability may vary seasonally and require reservations during peak times.

Gift shops and souvenir options

Yellowstone National Park offers a variety of gift shops and souvenir options to commemorate your visit and support the park's preservation efforts. Key locations for finding these shops include the Old Faithful Inn Gift Shop, located within the historic Old Faithful Inn, in Canyon Village, near the visitor center, Mammoth Hot Springs, in Lake Yellowstone, Grant Village, Tower-Roosevelt, in Fishing Bridge, West Yellowstone (outside the park), Yellowstone Forever Institute and Bookstores, operated by the nonprofit Yellowstone Forever, and online through the official Yellowstone National Park and Yellowstone Forever websites.

These shops offer a range of merchandise, including apparel, accessories, books, artwork, and unique items that celebrate the natural and cultural heritage of Yellowstone. The selection of items may vary by location and availability can change seasonally. The Fishing Bridge General Store in the Fishing Bridge area often includes a selection of Yellowstone-themed merchandise.

In addition to these gift shops, the park also features the Yellowstone Forever Institute and Bookstores, operated by the nonprofit organization, which offers educational materials, books, and unique items related to the park.

Nearby dining options outside the park

If you're seeking eating alternatives near Yellowstone National Park but outside of its limits, the town of West Yellowstone is a favorite destination for tourists, particularly since it's close to the park's West Entrance. Here are some local West Yellowstone eating options:

> ➤ Wild West Pizzeria is located at 14 Madison Ave, West Yellowstone, MT 59758.Cuisine: Pizza,

spaghetti, salads, and sandwiches in a family-friendly setting.

- ➤ 2. Running Bear Pancake House: - Location: 538 Madison Ave, West Yellowstone, MT 59758 - Cuisine: A renowned breakfast place that serves pancakes, waffles, omelets, and more.

- ➤ 3. Café Madriz: - Location: 310 Madison Ave, West Yellowstone, MT 59758 - Spanish cuisine includes tapas, paella, and a variety of foods.

- ➤ 4. Gusher Pizza and Sandwich Shoppe is located at 511 Scott St W, West Yellowstone, MT 59758.Cuisine: Pizza, sandwiches, and salads served in a calm, informal environment.

- ➤ 5. Bullwinkle's Saloon and Eatery is located at 115 N Canyon St, West Yellowstone, MT 59758.Cuisine: American pub-style cuisine, such as burgers, sandwiches, and substantial dinners.

- ➤ Blue Ribbon Cafe: - Address: 223 Canyon St, West Yellowstone, MT 59758 - Cuisine: A charming café serving breakfast and lunch, including sandwiches, soups, and baked goods.

- ➤ 7. Buffalo Bar: - Location: 335 US-20, West Yellowstone, MT 59758 - Cuisine: A typical Montana bar and grill with a menu that includes burgers, steaks, and substantial dishes.

- ➤ 8. The Branch Restaurant & Bar: - Address: 315 Yellowstone Ave, West Yellowstone, MT 59758 - Cuisine: A restaurant and bar with a broad menu including seafood, pasta, and trademark dishes.

- ➤ 9. The Fire hole BBQ Co. is located at 321 Electric St, West Yellowstone, MT 59758.Cuisine: A barbecue restaurant noted for its smoked meats, ribs, and tasty side dishes.

- ➤ 10. Ernie's Bakery and Deli is located at 7 Madison Ave, West Yellowstone, MT 59758.Cuisine: A bakery and deli serving sandwiches, pastries, and freshly baked items.

These are just a few alternatives in West Yellowstone, and you'll discover a wide range of cuisines and eating styles to fit your tastes. Keep in mind that restaurant availability and services may vary, so check current reviews and operating hours before arranging your visit.

CHAPTER 11: CULTURAL AND HISTORICAL INSIGHTS

Native American history and cultural significance

Yellowstone National Park is home to a rich history and cultural significance of Native American peoples. The Shoshone, Bannock, and Sheepeater tribes, who historically inhabited the region, had a rich cultural heritage tied to the land's resources, including bison, fish, and plants. Their traditional land use included sustainable practices like hunting, fishing, and gathering, with bison playing a crucial role in their way of life.

The Yellowstone region contains sacred sites for various tribes, which hold spiritual significance and are connected to creation stories and cultural practices. The Lewis and Clark Expedition (1804-1806) marked early contact between Euro-American explorers and Native American communities. The fur trade era brought European Americans into the region, leading to increased interactions with Native American communities.

The Oregon Trail and Indigenous Displacement led to displacement and conflicts with Indigenous peoples. The Fort Laramie Treaties of 1851 and 1868 were significant agreements between the U.S. government and various tribes but were often violated, leading to further displacement.

Despite historical challenges, Native American communities continue to preserve and revitalize their cultures through language revitalization, traditional ceremonies, and community events. The present-day significance of Yellowstone National Park lies in its collaborations with Native American tribes on initiatives that recognize and respect tribal perspectives, incorporate traditional ecological knowledge, and address shared concerns about the park's resources. The National Park Service engages in tribal consultation processes to involve Indigenous communities in park management decisions and ensure their cultural perspectives are considered.

Understanding the Native American history and cultural significance in Yellowstone requires recognizing the diversity of Indigenous perspectives and acknowledging the ongoing contributions of Native American communities to the region's heritage.

Historical sites within the park

Yellowstone National Park is renowned for its stunning natural landscapes, geothermal features, and diverse wildlife. However, the park also boasts several historical sites that reflect human history and past activities. Notable sites include the Fort Yellowstone Historic District, established in 1886 by the U.S. Army, which houses several historic structures from this era. The Norris Geyser Basin Museum, built in 1929, is an early National Park Service rustic architecture museum and visitor center. The Old Faithful Inn, built in 1903-1904, is an iconic symbol of Yellowstone and a historic site.

The Haynes Photo Shop, operated by the Haynes family, dates back to 1910 and played a significant role in promoting Yellowstone through photography and early tourism. The Yellowstone Lake Hotel, built in 1891, is one of the oldest and most elegant structures in the park, with Colonial Revival architecture reflecting early efforts to provide upscale accommodations.

The Lake Fish Hatchery, constructed in 1903, was part of an effort to stock non-native fish species in Yellowstone Lake. The Roosevelt Lodge, built in 1920, is a historic cabin-style lodge named after

President Theodore Roosevelt, reflecting the rustic architecture popular in the early 20th century. The Tower Fall Area features remnants of the original Tower Falls General Store, built in 1890, which served as a trading post during the military administration. These historical sites showcase the evolution of Yellowstone National Park from its early years to the development of visitor services and the establishment of the National Park Service.

Preservation efforts and initiatives

Yellowstone National Park, established in 1872 as the world's first national park, has been a center for preservation efforts since its inception. The National Park Service (NPS) was created in 1916 to oversee and manage the park, playing a crucial role in preserving and protecting its resources.

Key conservation and wildlife efforts include the conservation of the park's iconic bison herds, the reintroduction of gray wolves in 1995 and 1996, and the management of grizzly bear populations. Fire management involves allowing natural fire regimes to play their ecological role, with controlled burns and monitoring used to manage fire impacts while maintaining ecosystem health. Boardwalks and infrastructure are constructed around geothermal features to protect visitors and the delicate thermal ecosystems. Geothermal monitoring helps track changes in thermal areas, ensuring their preservation and understanding the dynamic nature of these unique environments.

Cultural resource preservation includes the Fort Yellowstone Historic District, which focuses on maintaining and protecting historic structures for future generations. Collaborative efforts with Native American tribes aim to respect and incorporate Indigenous perspectives in park management decisions. Sustainable tourism initiatives include visitor education, transportation initiatives, and Leave No Trace principles.

Research and monitoring are essential for understanding ecological processes, wildlife behavior, and climate change impacts, as well as tracking changes in the park's ecosystems. Yellowstone is actively engaged in adaptive management strategies to address the impacts of climate change on the park's ecosystems, including altered precipitation patterns, temperature changes, and shifting wildlife habitats.

Preservation efforts in Yellowstone are dynamic and continually evolving to address new challenges and opportunities, reflecting a commitment to maintaining the park's ecological integrity, preserving its cultural heritage, and ensuring that future generations can experience the wonders of Yellowstone National Park.

CHAPTER 12: SAFETY AND REGULATIONS

Emergency contacts and services

At the event of an emergency at Yellowstone National Park, access to emergency contacts and services is critical. Here are key connections and services in the park:

Emergency services:

> ➤ In case of an emergency, call 911. This number may link you to emergency services such as medical help, fire, and police enforcement.

> ➤ 2. Yellowstone National Park has its own emergency services. Please contact the park's emergency services for help.

> ➤ 3. Ranger Stations: - Rangers are stationed around the park and may provide aid during crises. Determine the location of the closest ranger station.

Medical Assistance:

> ➤ Yellowstone National Park has medical facilities in certain locations. Check the availability and location of clinics for non-emergency medical issues.

> ➤

> ➤ 2. Yellowstone Medical facility: Located near Mammoth Hot Springs, this facility offers medical services to both park tourists and inhabitants. Contact them if you have any non-emergency medical problems.

Search and rescue:

> ➤ Search and Rescue (SAR):- In case of a search and rescue, call park officials or phone 911 for help.

> ➤ 2. Backcountry Emergencies: If you're in the wilderness and need help, use a whistle, signal mirror, or other signaling devices to attract attention. Carry a communication device if feasible.

Park Information:

➤ Contact Park Dispatch for general park information or to report non-emergency issues.

➤ 2. Visitor Centers: - Located throughout the park, visitor centers provide information on services, conditions, and safety.

Road Condition:

➤ Road Information: - Check road conditions and closures before traveling. Road conditions may have an influence on park travel.

➤ 2. Yellowstone National Park's road status hotline provides current information on road conditions.

Wildlife Safety:

> ➤ When encountering a bear, keep a safe distance and avoid approaching. In the event of a bear encounter, notify park officials.

> ➤ 2. To ensure safe animal watching, follow these precautions. Maintain a safe distance and use binoculars or telephoto lenses to get close-up views.

Important Tips:

> ➤ Stay updated about current conditions, weather predictions, and park alerts/warnings.

> ➤ 2. Be Prepared: - Bring basics like water, food, clothes, maps, and a first aid kit. If you're going into the wilderness, let someone know your plans.

➢ 3. Cell Phone coverage: - Some portions of the park may have poor coverage. Be aware of where you may get a signal and prepare appropriately.

➢ 4. Follow park laws for animal watching, camping, and other activities.

➢ 5. Practice Leave No Trace principles to minimize environmental harm and maintain the park for future generations.

When visiting Yellowstone National Park, always place safety first. To guarantee a safe and pleasurable visit, familiarize yourself with emergency contact information, be prepared for varied weather, and adhere to park standards.

Safety guidelines for different activities

Yellowstone National Park offers a variety of activities, each with its own set of safety considerations. These include hiking, wildlife viewing, boating and fishing, camping, winter activities, geothermal features, road safety, and staying back.

Hiking involves sticking to designated trails to protect fragile ecosystems and avoid getting lost. Bear spray is essential in a bear country, and bear awareness is crucial. Be aware of trail conditions, including weather forecasts and closures. Weather preparedness involves dressing in layers and carrying essentials like water, snacks, a map, and a first aid kit.

Weather preparedness involves dressing in layers and carrying essentials like water, snacks, a map, and a first aid kit. It is important to inform others about your hiking plans and expected return time. Wildlife viewing involves using binoculars and telephoto lenses to keep a safe distance from wildlife, staying in your vehicle, not feeding wildlife, and avoiding crowding.

Boating and fishing regulations require adhering to park regulations, wearing life jackets, checking weather conditions, following fishing regulations, and preventing aquatic invasive species. Camping requires respecting campsite regulations, properly storing food, following fire regulations, and leaving no trace.

Winter activities involve dressing appropriately, carrying essential gear, and being aware of avalanche conditions.

In remote or backcountry areas, it is essential to leave trash and minimize environmental impact.

Geothermal features require sticking to designated paths, obeying warning signs, keeping pets on leashes, and maintaining a safe distance from thermal features. Road safety involves following speed limits, watching for wildlife, pulling over safely, and driving cautiously. Always check with park rangers for the latest safety information and guidelines before engaging in any activities.

Park regulations and rules

Yellowstone National Park has a set of regulations and rules in place to ensure the safety of visitors, protect its natural and cultural resources, and preserve its unique ecosystem. These regulations include general rules such as paying the required entrance fee, adhering to operating hours, keeping pets on a leash, maintaining a safe distance from wildlife, practicing Leave No Trace principles, camping only in designated campsites, obtaining backcountry permits, and following fishing regulations.

Safety rules include emergency procedures, staying on boardwalks and designated trails near geothermal features, observing speed limits, being cautious of wildlife on roads, carrying bear spray, respecting Native American sites, special use permits for events and filming, research permits, winter safety, snowmobile and snow coach regulations, boating regulations, commercial use authorizations for tour operators, and educational programs and permits for educational groups.

Emergency procedures include knowing emergency procedures and contacts, dialing 911 for emergencies, staying on established trails, being aware of avalanche conditions, respecting Native American sites, and obtaining special use permits for events, commercial filming, and research. Winter safety involves being prepared for winter conditions, carrying appropriate gear and clothing, and checking road and trail conditions. Snowmobile and snow coach regulations require specific regulations for use in the park while boating regulations require permits for boating on Yellowstone Lake and other bodies of water.

Commercial use authorizations are required for commercial tour operators and educational groups. Visitors need to check with park rangers for the most up-to-date information on regulations and rules, as they may change based on current conditions or new initiatives. Adhering to these regulations ensures the protection of Yellowstone National Park for future generations.

CHAPTER 13: TRAVEL TIPS

Entrance fees and passes

The admission fees and permits for Yellowstone National Park were as follows. Please keep in mind that costs and pass information are subject to change, therefore the most up-to-date information may be found on the official Yellowstone National Park website or by contacting the park directly.

Entrance Fees for Private Vehicles:

➤ For private, non-commercial cars with a capacity of 15 people or fewer, a 7-day permit is $35 (per vehicle).

➤ Motorcycles: $30 for a 7-day ticket (per motorbike).

➤ Entrance Fees for Individuals (Pedestrians, Cyclists, and Non-Commercial Groups)

➤ Per Person (16 years and older): - $20 for a 7-day pass (per person).

Annual Passes:

> ➢ Yellowstone National Park offers an annual pass for $70 that is good for one year from the purchase date.
>
> ➢ America's Beautiful Passes

> ➢ The America the Beautiful National Parks and Federal Recreational Lands Annual Pass costs $80 and is good for one year from the purchase date.

> ➢ Senior Pass: - $80 for America the Beautiful National Parks and Federal Recreational Lands Senior Pass (lifetime pass for U.S. citizens or permanent residents aged 62 and over).

> ➢ The America the Beautiful National Parks and Federal Recreational Lands Access Pass is available for free to U.S. citizens or permanent residents with permanent impairments.

> ➢ Every Kid Outdoors Pass: is free. Fourth graders are eligible for a free Every Kid Outdoors Pass, which grants free access

to federal lands and waterways for the student and their families.

Special Programs:

➢ Military Annual Pass: - Free for active-duty U.S. military members and their families. Must be acquired in person at a federal recreation facility by presenting a Common Access Card (CAC) or Military ID (Form 1173).

➢ Volunteer Pass: - Free for volunteers with 250 cumulative service hours.

Important Notes:

Entrance fees are valid for seven days from the purchase date. Interagency passes, such as the America the Beautiful Pass, are also valid in Yellowstone National Park and other federal recreation areas.

Guided tours and ranger programs

It offers a variety of guided tours and ranger programs to enhance visitors' experiences and provide educational opportunities. These programs are led by knowledgeable park rangers and guides, allowing visitors to explore the park's unique features, wildlife, and cultural history. The availability of these programs may vary by season, so it is advisable to check with the park's visitor centers for the latest information.

Some common ranger-led programs include geological and naturalist talks, wildlife viewing programs, historical interpretation, and night sky programs. Guided tours include bus tours, snow coach tours (winter), boat tours, hiking tours, and specialized programs like photography tours and Yellowstone Institute programs.

Customized tours and private ranger-guided tours are also available, allowing visitors to tailor their experiences based on specific interests and preferences. Some private tour company's offer customized tours, while others require reservations, especially during peak visitation times. Lodges within the park may offer guided tours or have information on available programs.

To participate in these programs, visitors can inquire at visitor centers, make online reservations, or visit Yellowstone National Park lodges. Participating in these programs provides an excellent way to gain deeper insights into the natural and cultural wonders of Yellowstone while enjoying the expertise of knowledgeable guides.

Accessibility information

Yellowstone National Park is dedicated to ensuring accessibility for visitors with disabilities. The park offers various facilities and accommodations, including wheelchair-accessible visitor centers, restrooms, lodging options, trails and boardwalks, ranger-led programs, assistive listening devices, and Braille materials. Visitors can check with park rangers or visitor centers for information on accessible trails and boardwalks.

Some ranger-led programs and talks are wheelchair accessible, and some may provide assistive listening devices. Braille materials may also be available for informational materials. Accessible transportation options are available through some tour operators, and designated parking spaces are available at various locations.

For planning, visitors can visit the official Yellowstone National Park website for information on accessibility features and services. If they have specific accessibility concerns or questions, they can contact the park directly, and some parks offer accessibility maps that highlight features and routes. Service animals are generally allowed in national parks, but they must comply with park regulations.

The park covers a vast area with diverse terrain, and not all areas may be fully accessible. It is advisable to inquire about specific needs when planning your visit and check for updates or changes to accessibility features.

Navigation tips for popular attractions

Offers a vast array of attractions, making it an exciting adventure for visitors. To navigate the park, follow these tips:

1. Start with a detailed park map, available at entrance stations, visitor centers, and online. Familiarize yourself with the park's layout, key features, and road network.

2. Plan visits to iconic areas like Old Faithful, Grand Prismatic Spring, and Norris Geyser Basin using boardwalks.

3. Enjoy wildlife viewing in Lamar Valley, known for its wolves and bison. Remember to follow wildlife safety guidelines and bring binoculars for better viewing.

4. Visit Canyon Village, the Grand Canyon of the Yellowstone, offering hiking trails and stunning viewpoints.

5. Explore Lake Area, the largest high-elevation lake in North America, and explore the Lake Village area.

6. Visit Mammoth Hot Springs, located near the park's north entrance, featuring colorful mineral formations and the historic Fort Yellowstone.

7. Visit the Tower-Roosevelt Area, known for its waterfall and wildlife, including bison and pronghorn.

8. Explore Old Faithful, one of the most famous geysers, and take advantage of predicted eruption times.

9. Visit visitor centers for information, maps, and ranger-led programs.

10. Check weather and road conditions, especially during shoulder seasons, as some roads may be closed during winter.

11. Plan based on interests and time available, being mindful of distances between attractions.

13. Be patient, follow traffic rules, and use pullouts to enjoy views and wildlife safely.

14. Join ranger programs for in-depth insights into the park's natural and cultural wonders.

15. Consider visiting popular attractions during sunrise or sunset for beautiful lighting and fewer crowds.

16. Research and plan hiking trails based on skill level and interests, as many lead to spectacular viewpoints.

18. Respect park regulations, including speed limits, wildlife viewing guidelines, and Leave No Trace principles.

19. Check for alerts before your visit to ensure your safety.

Conclusion

Yellowstone National Park is a breathtaking natural wonder with stunning landscapes, geothermal wonders, and diverse wildlife. Its unique features, such as the erupting geysers of Old Faithful and the Grand Canyon of Yellowstone, reveal new chapters in the planet's natural history. The park's diverse wildlife, including bison, wolves, and grizzly bears, adds a dynamic dimension to the experience. Visitors can explore the geothermal areas, scenic drives, or ranger-led programs. However, it's crucial to follow park regulations, prioritize safety, and practice responsible tourism principles. Yellowstone's delicate ecosystems deserve our respect and protection to ensure future generations can enjoy its wonders. In conclusion, Yellowstone National Park is a living testament to conservation, education, and the enduring power of the natural world. It invites visitors to become part of its story, leaving an indelible mark on those fortunate enough to experience its magic.

Made in United States
Troutdale, OR
09/17/2024